This Book Belongs To

COLOR TEST PAGES

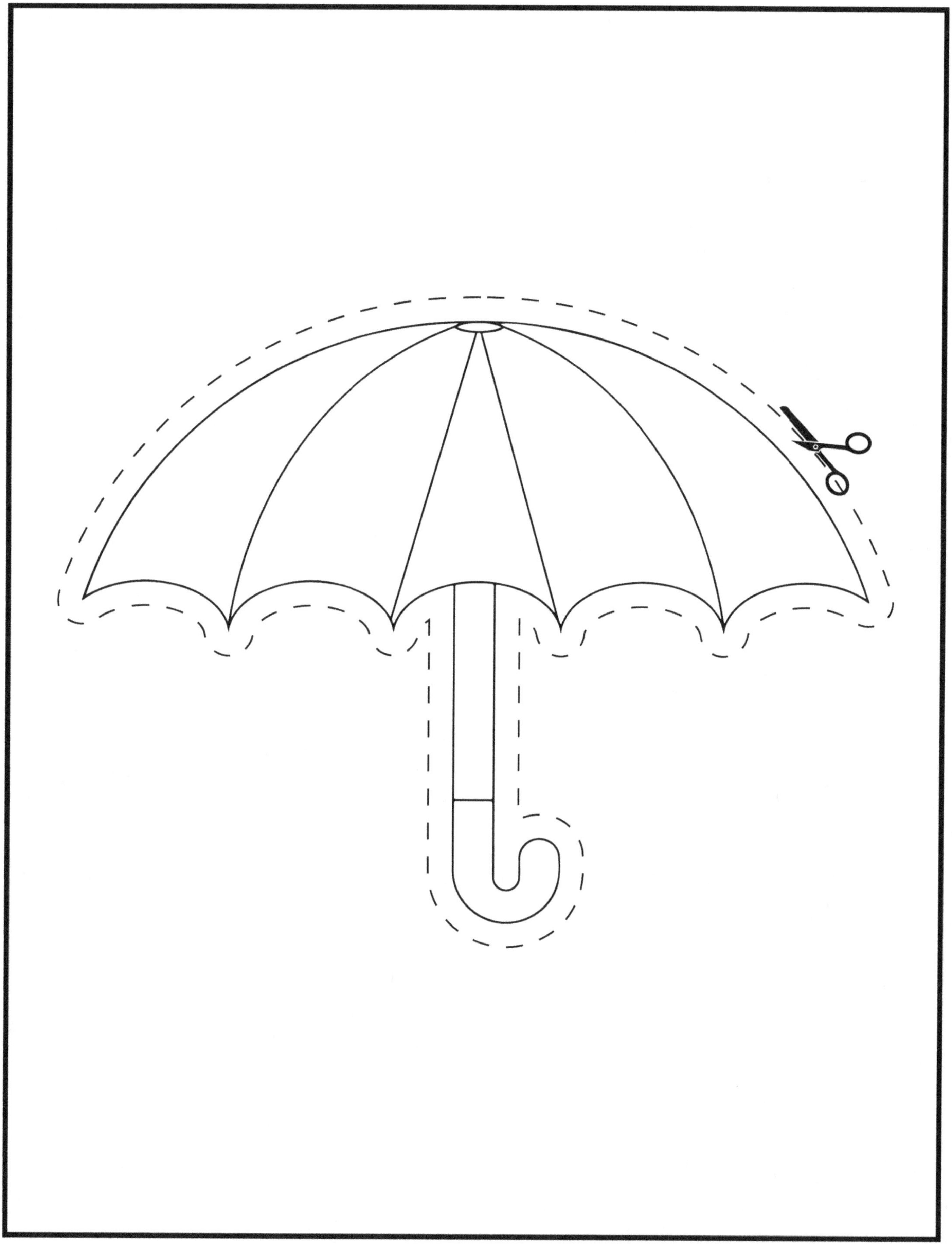

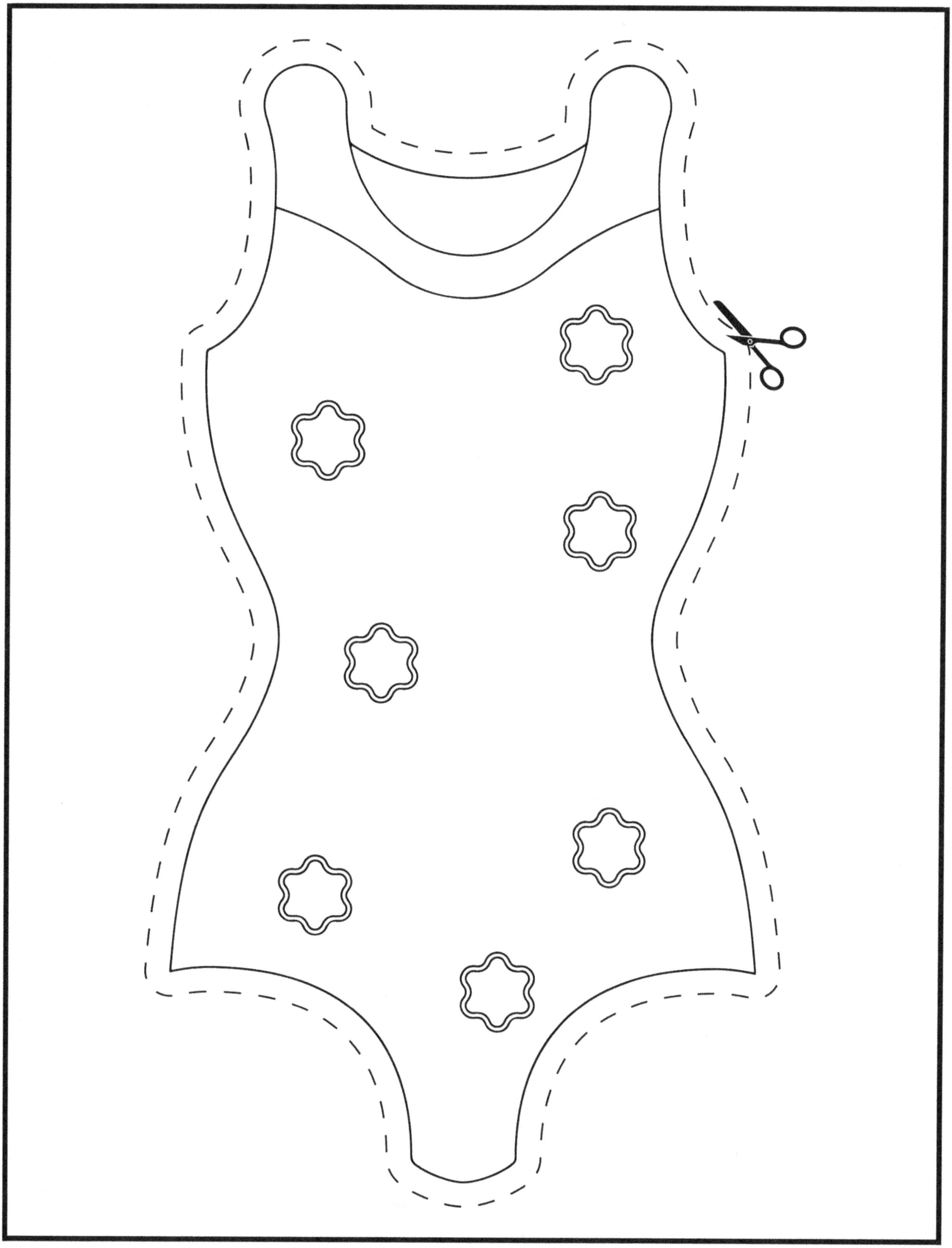

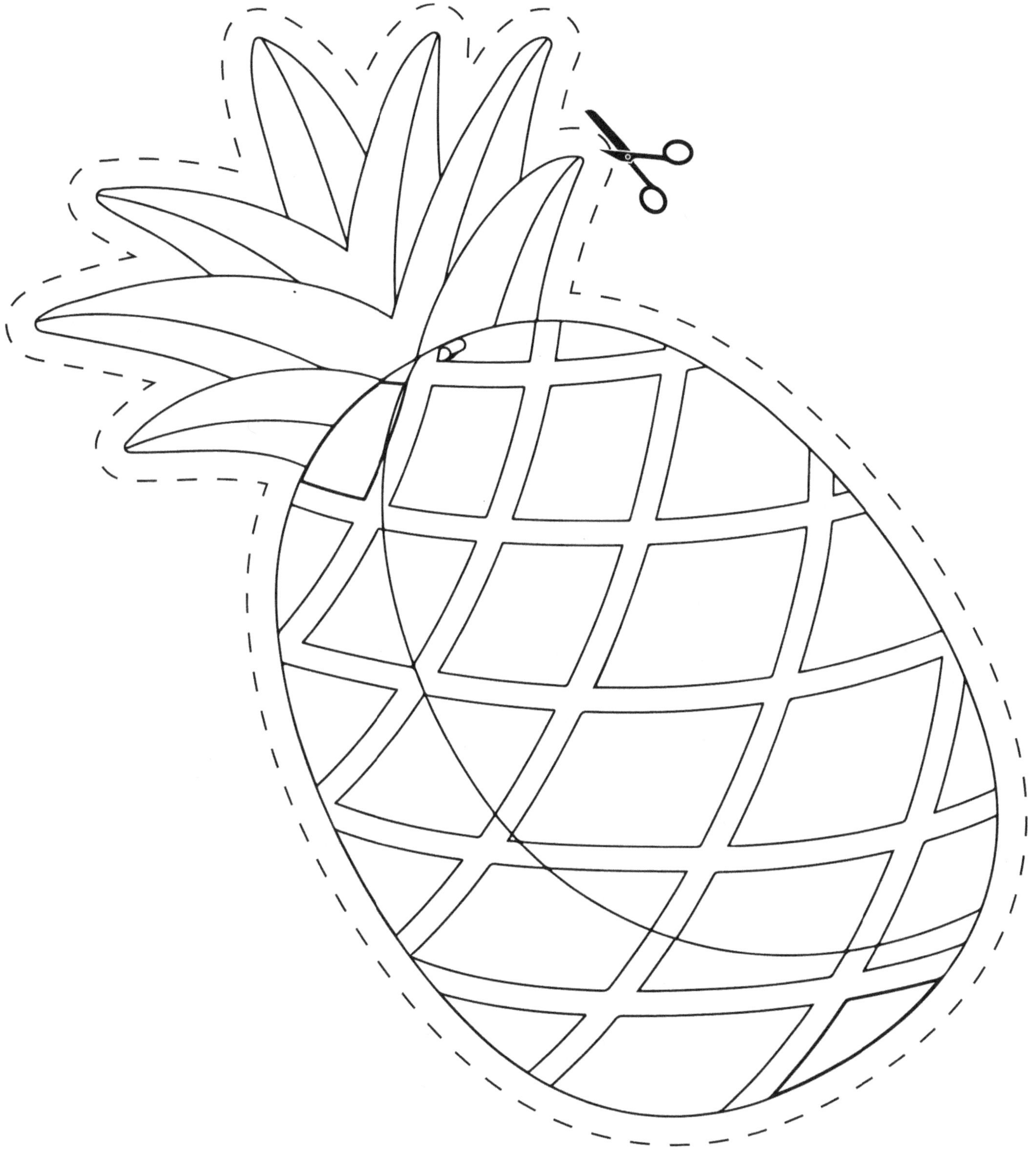

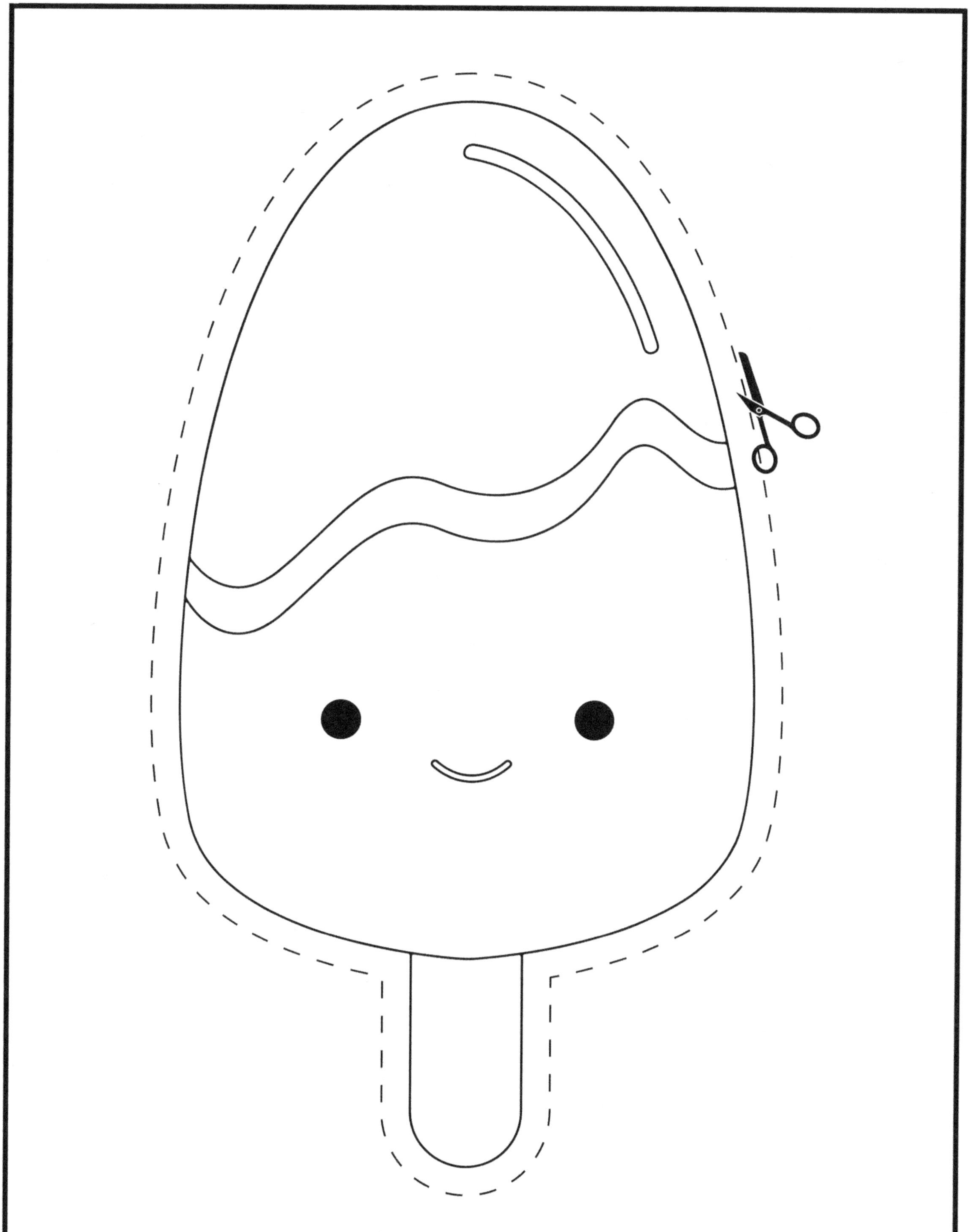

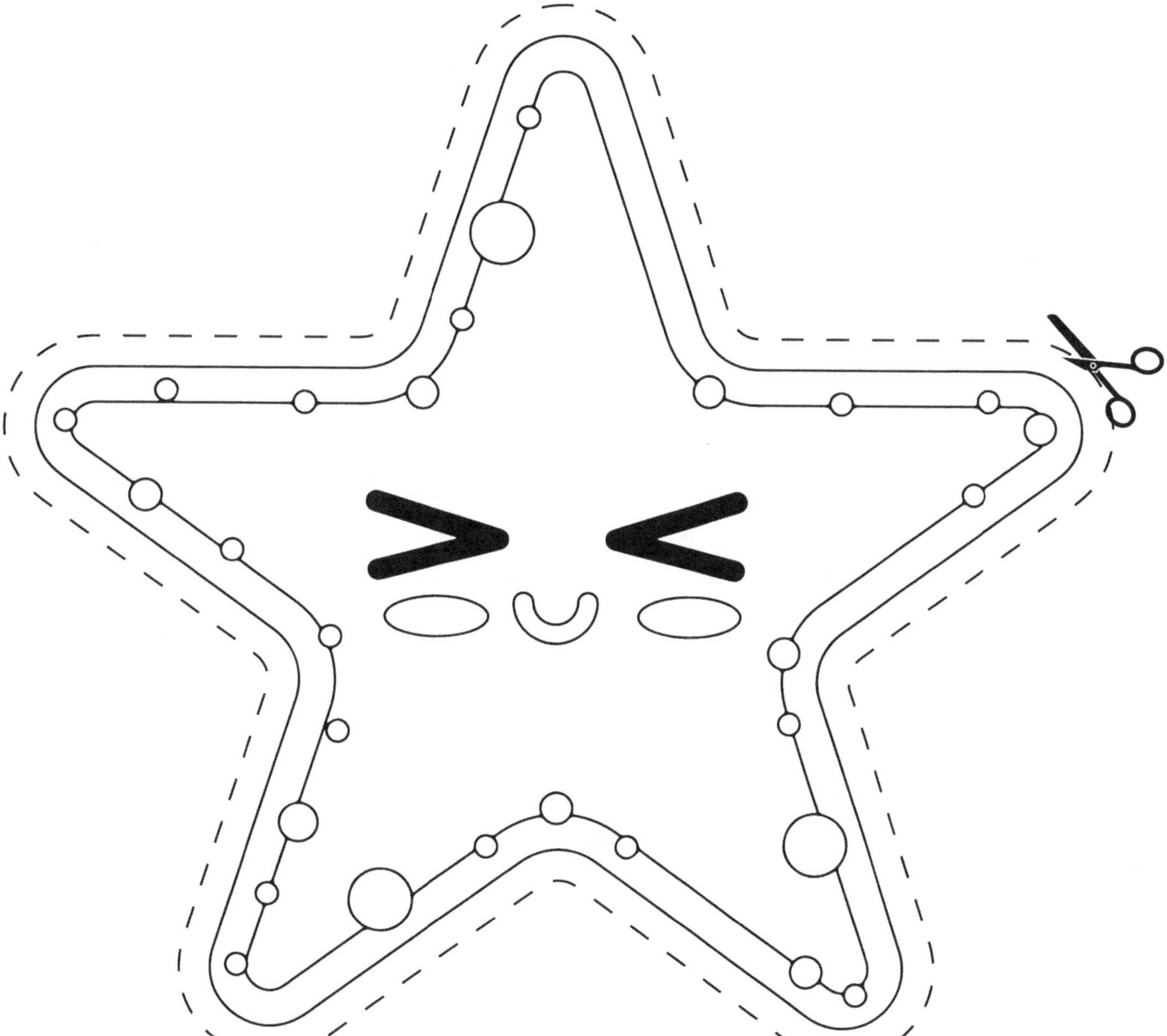

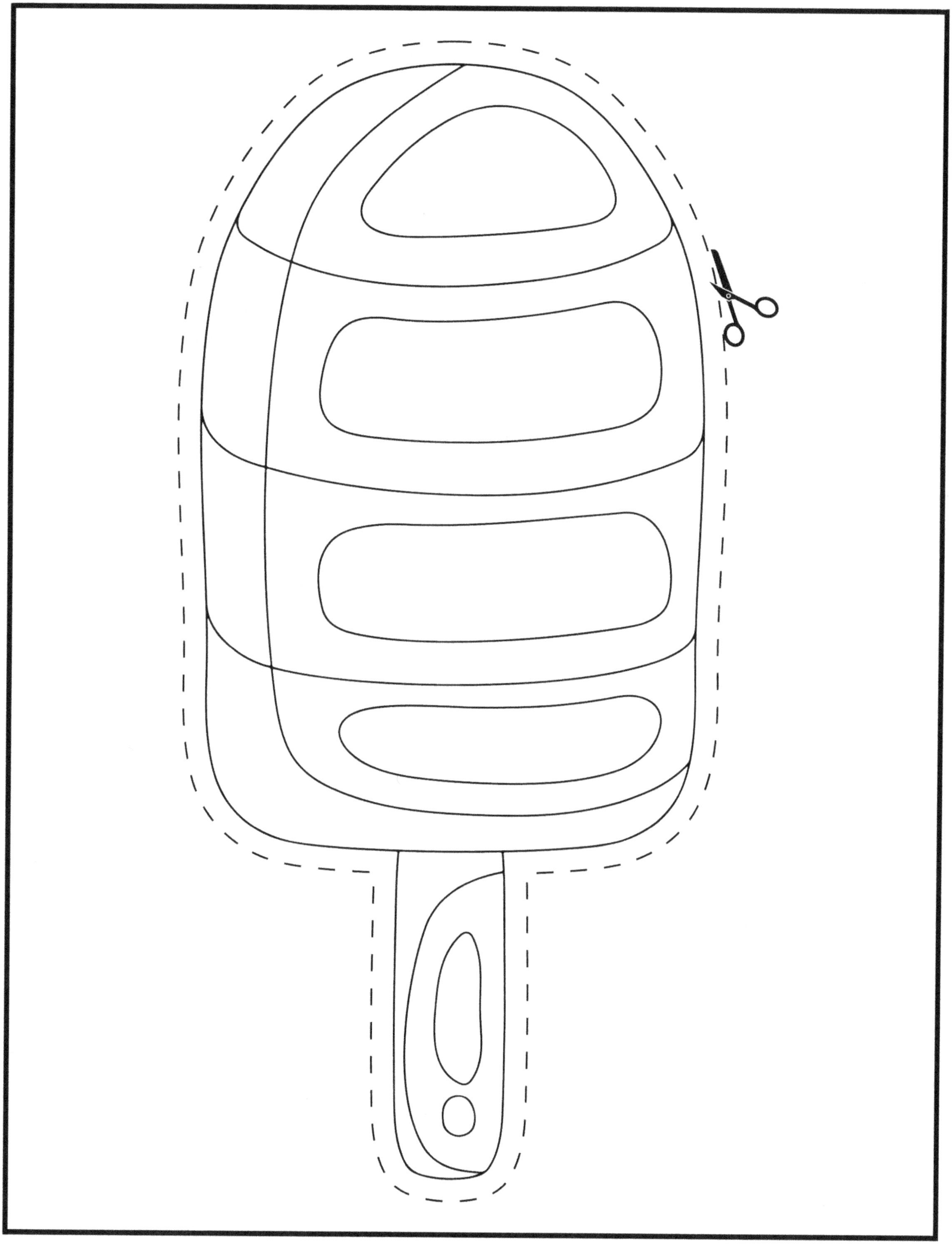

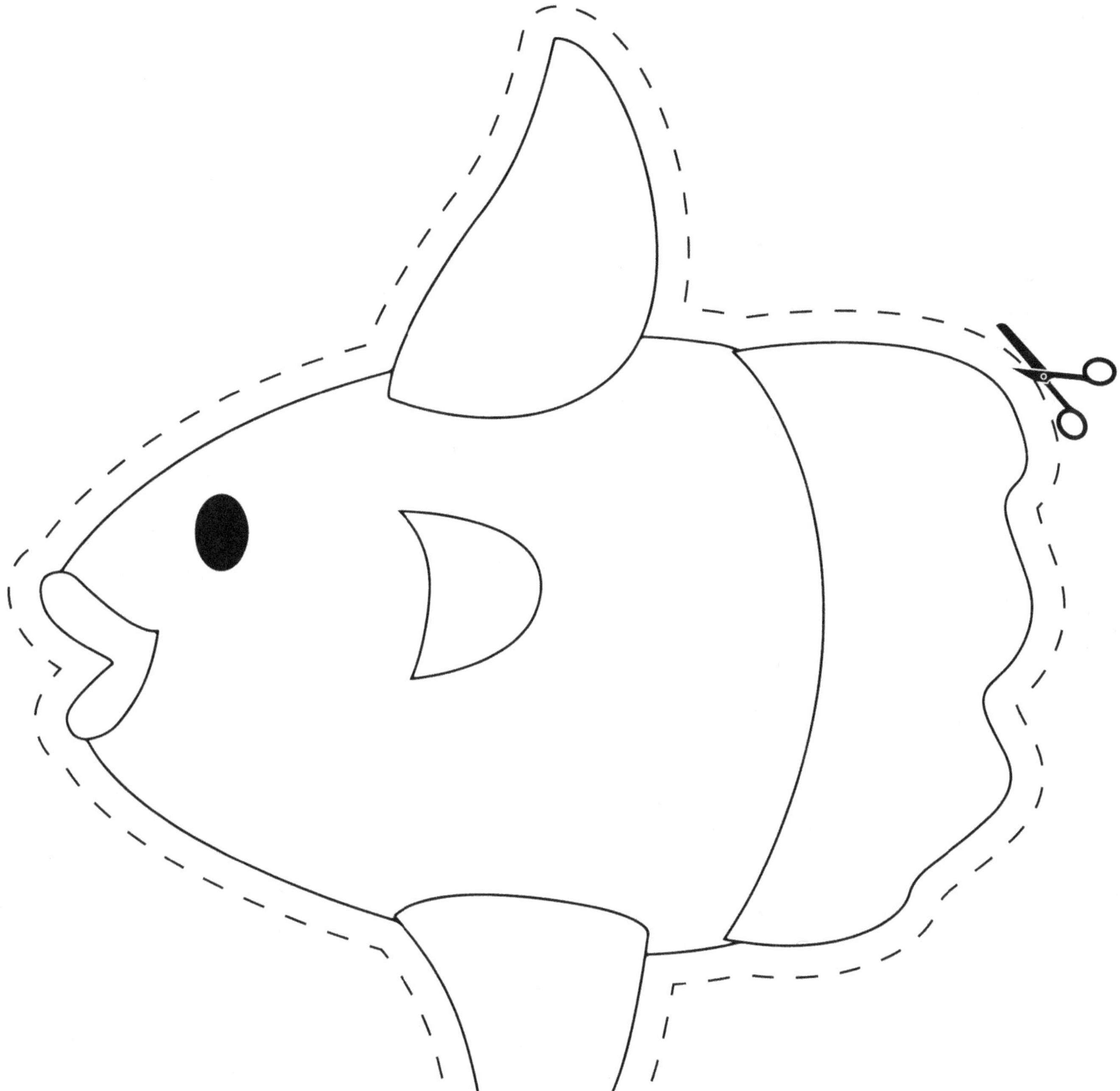

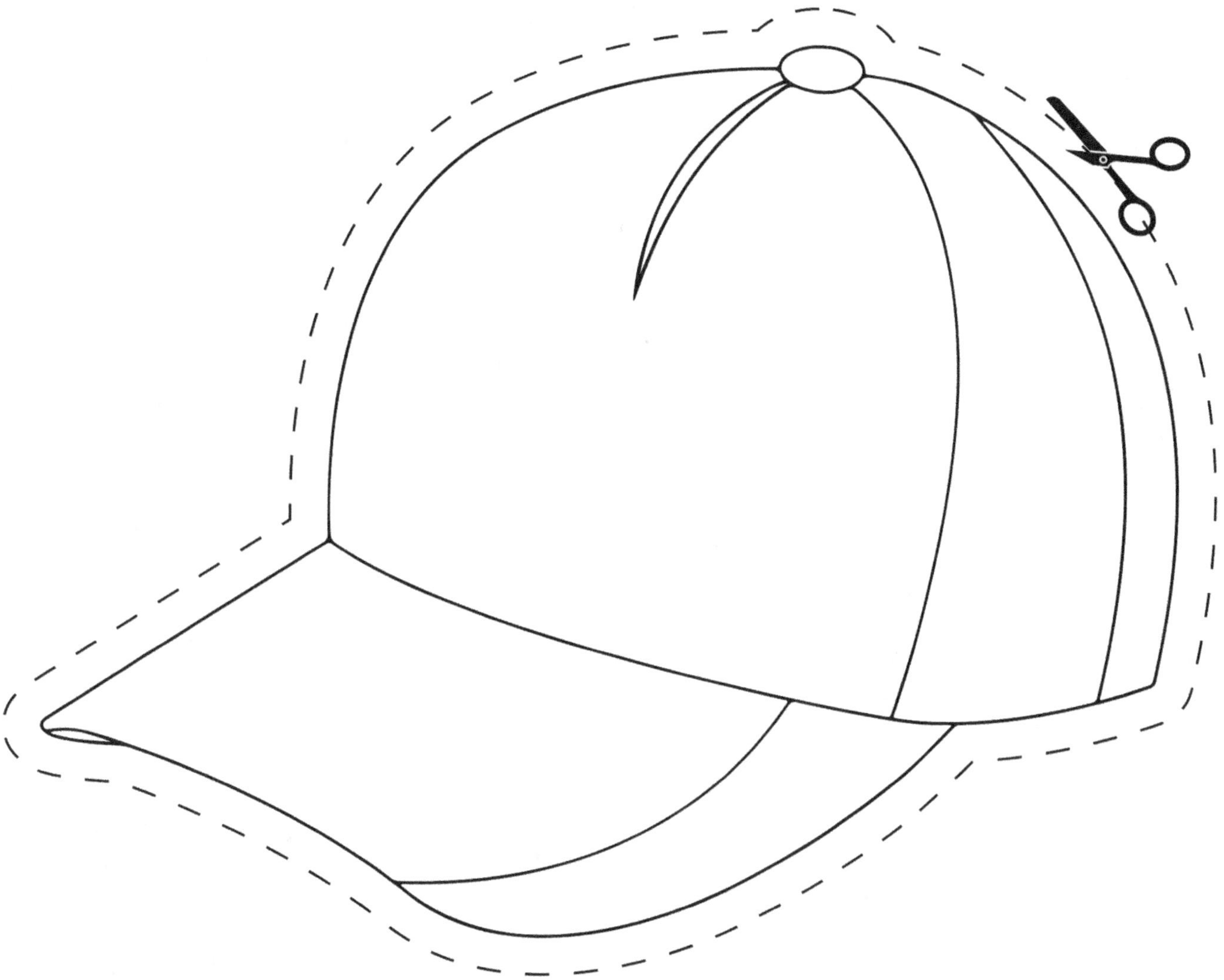

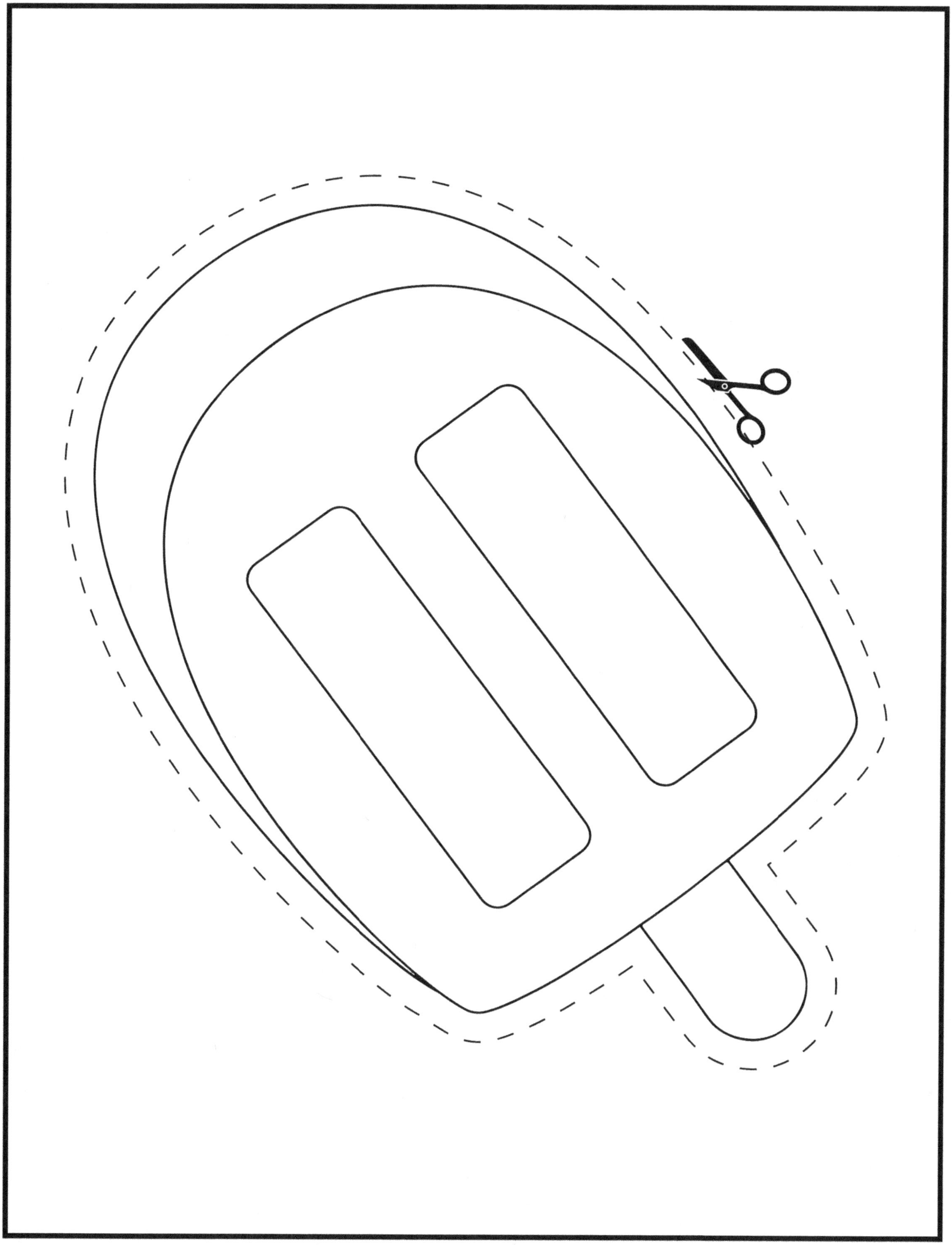

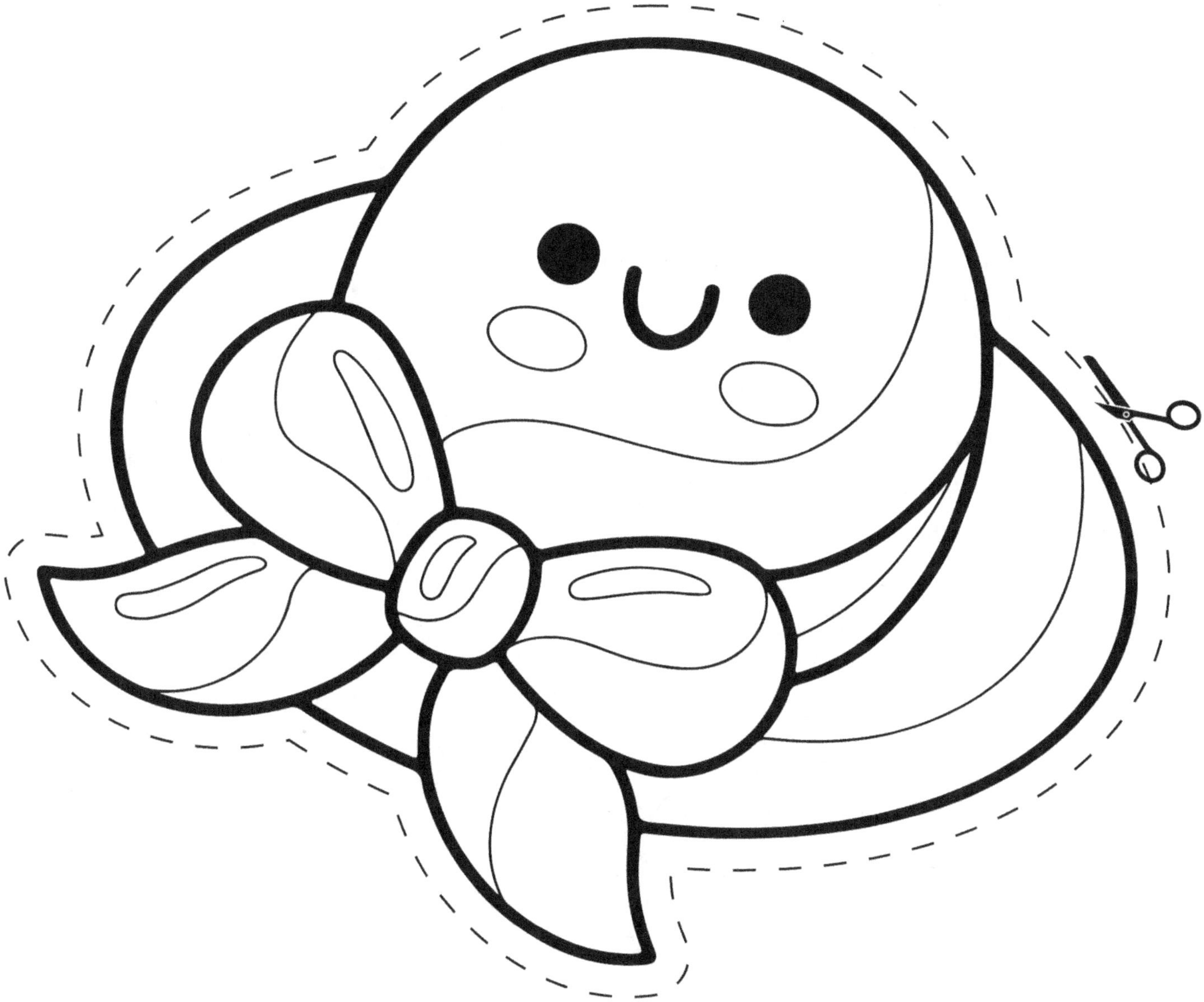

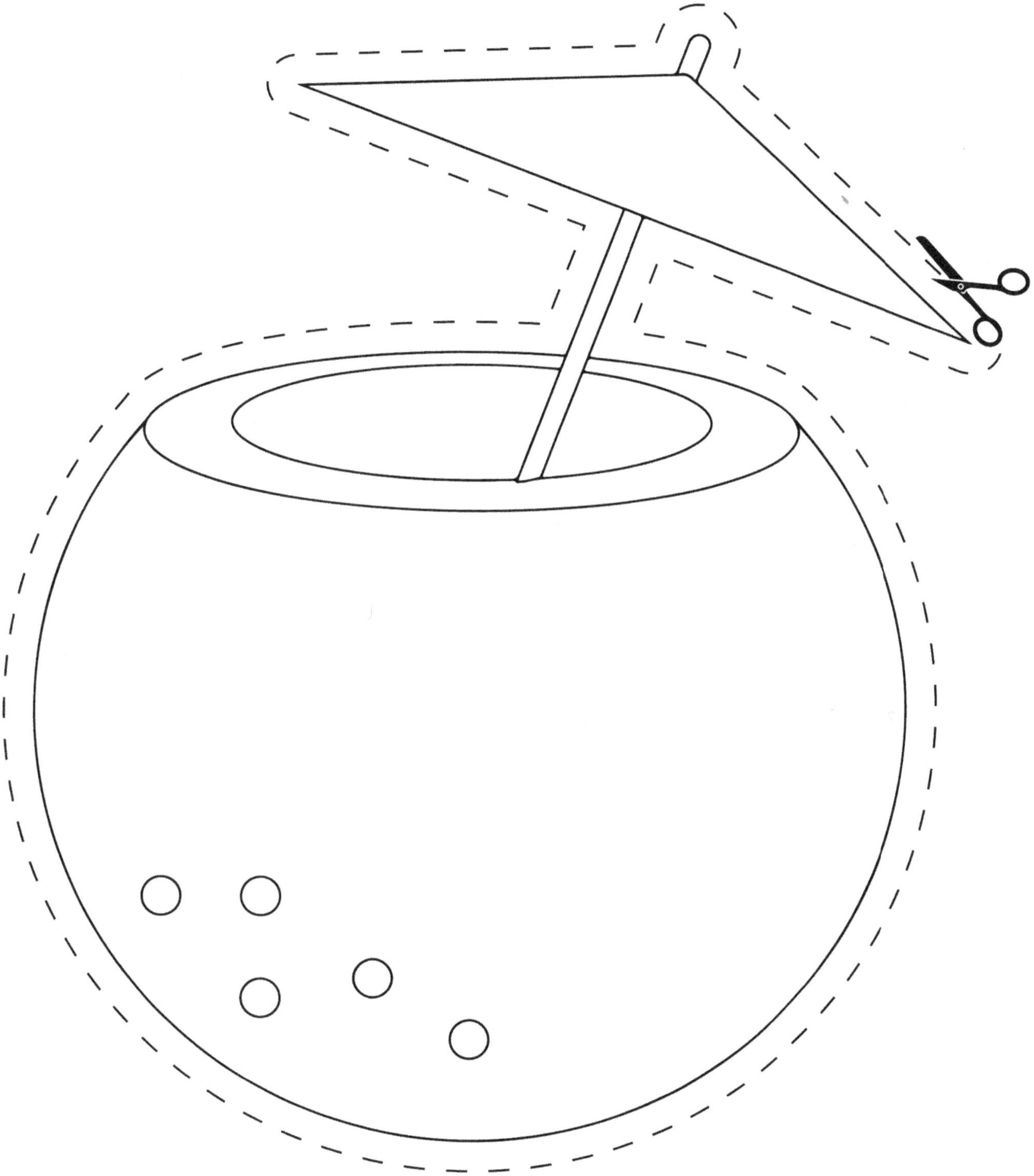

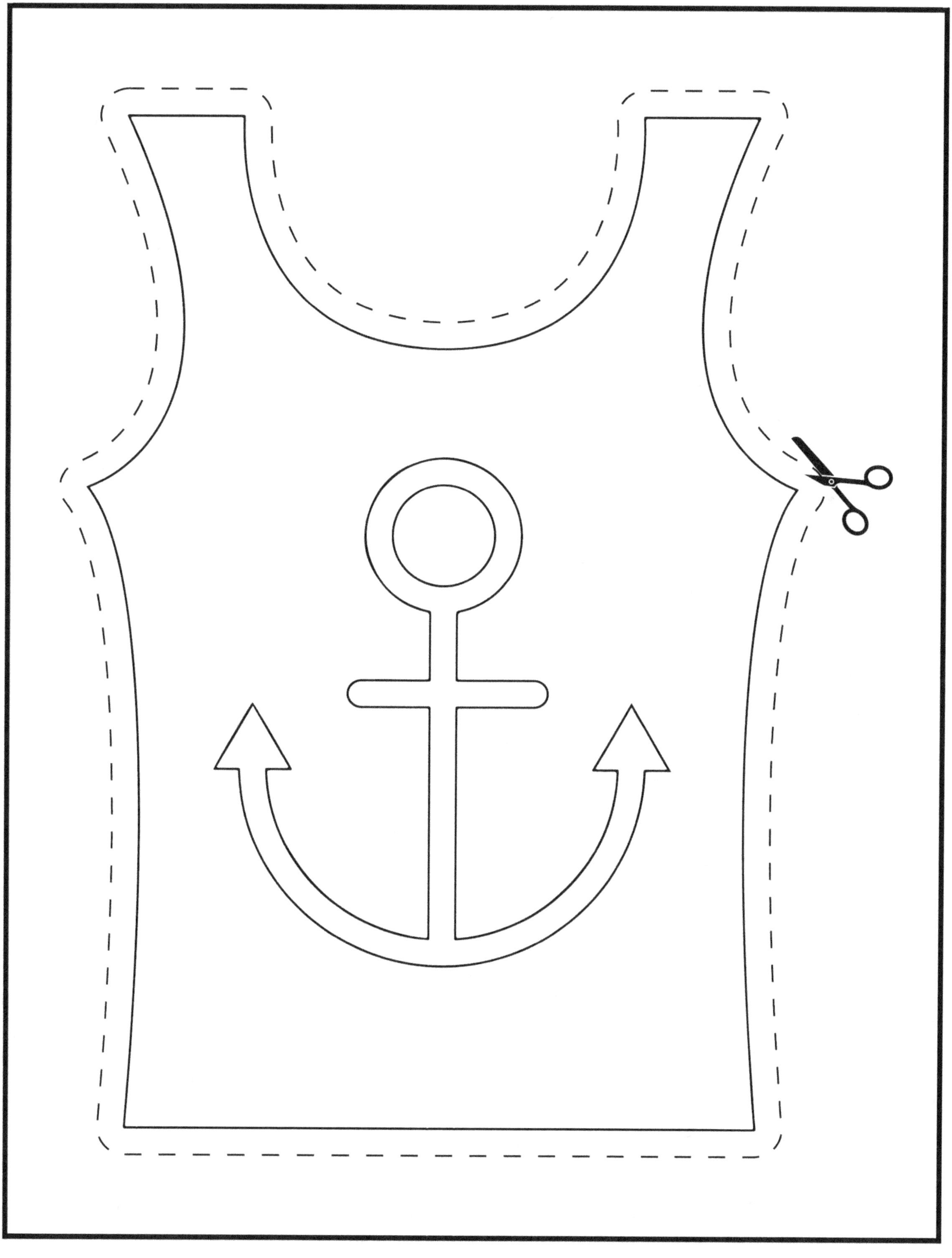

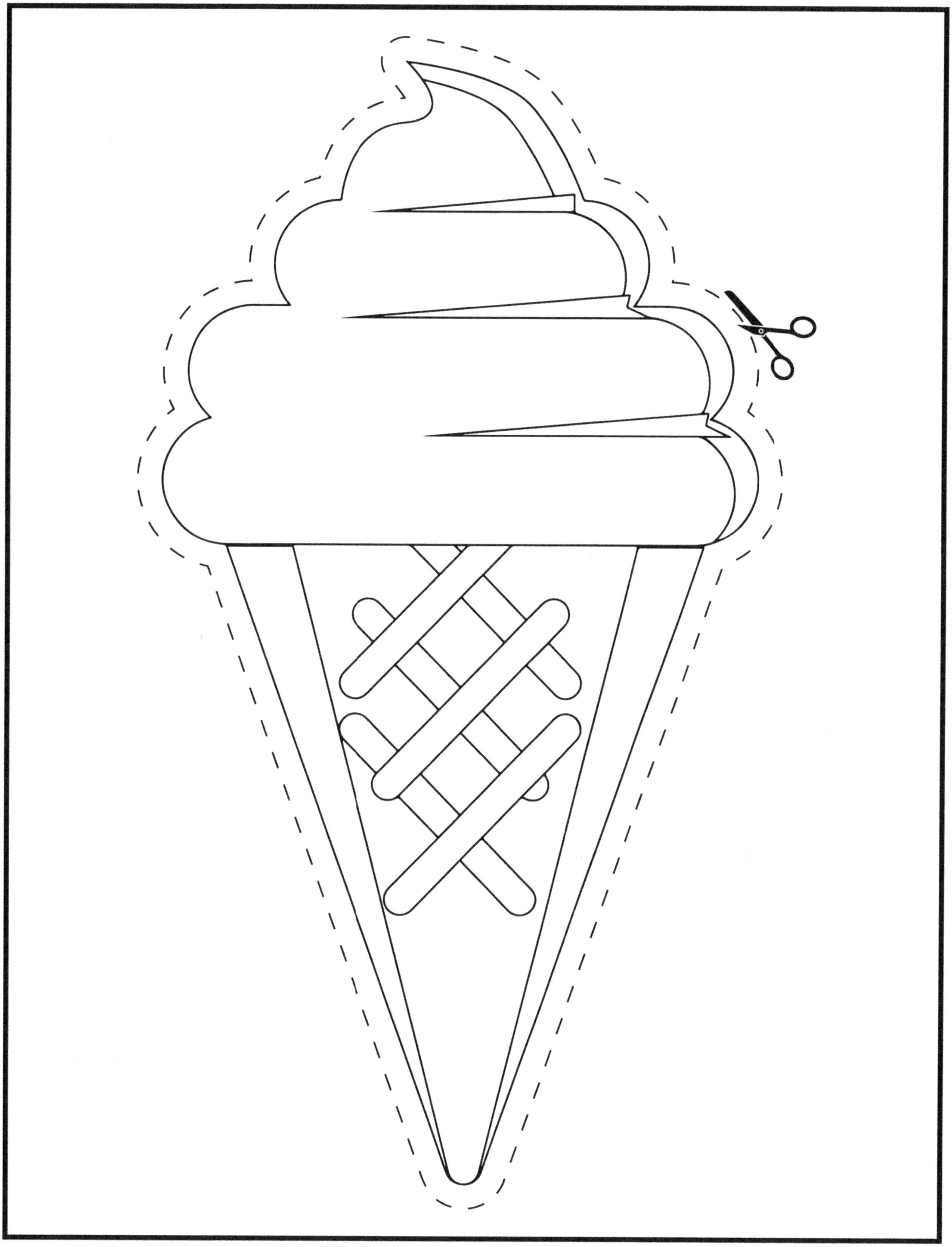

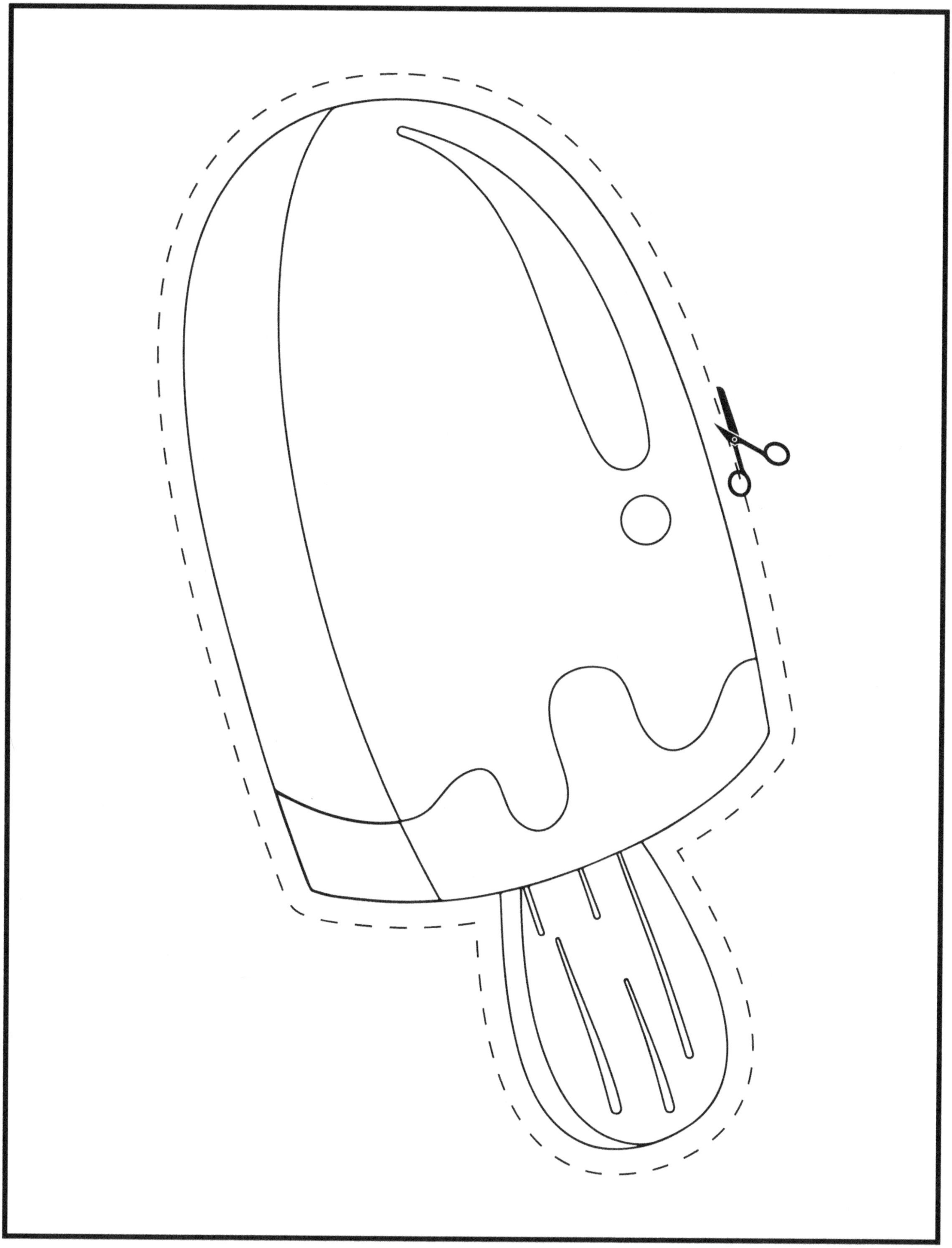

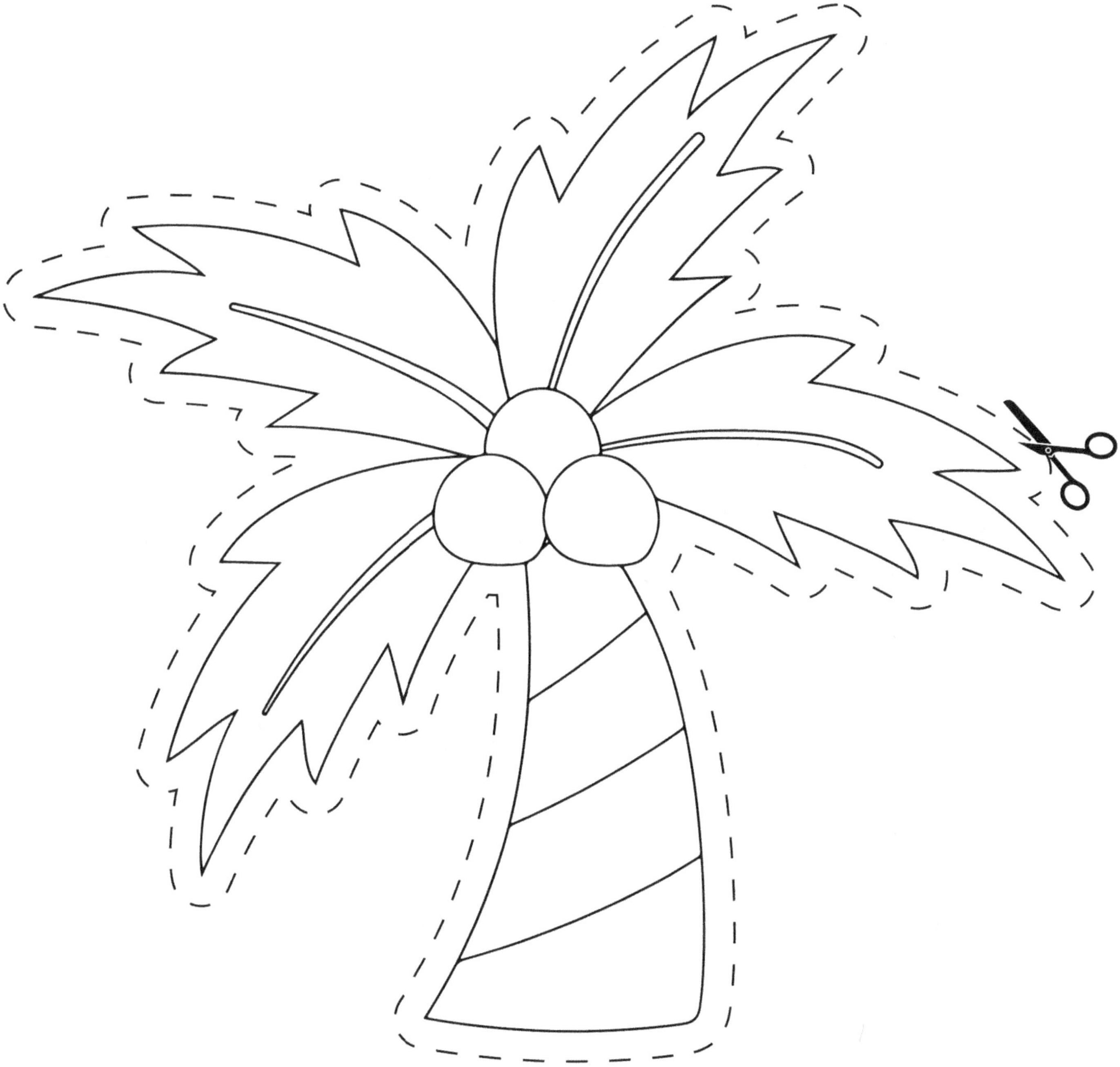

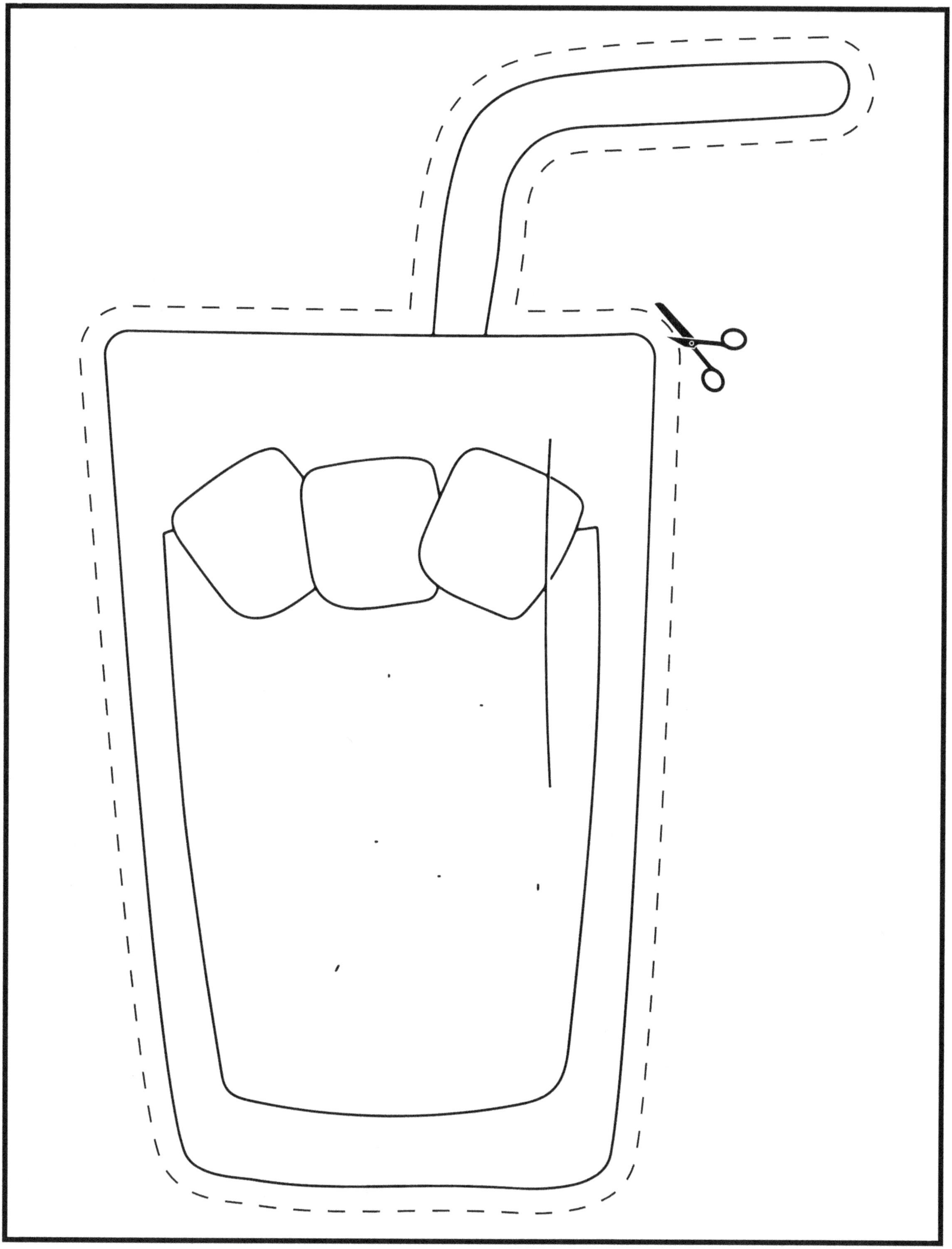

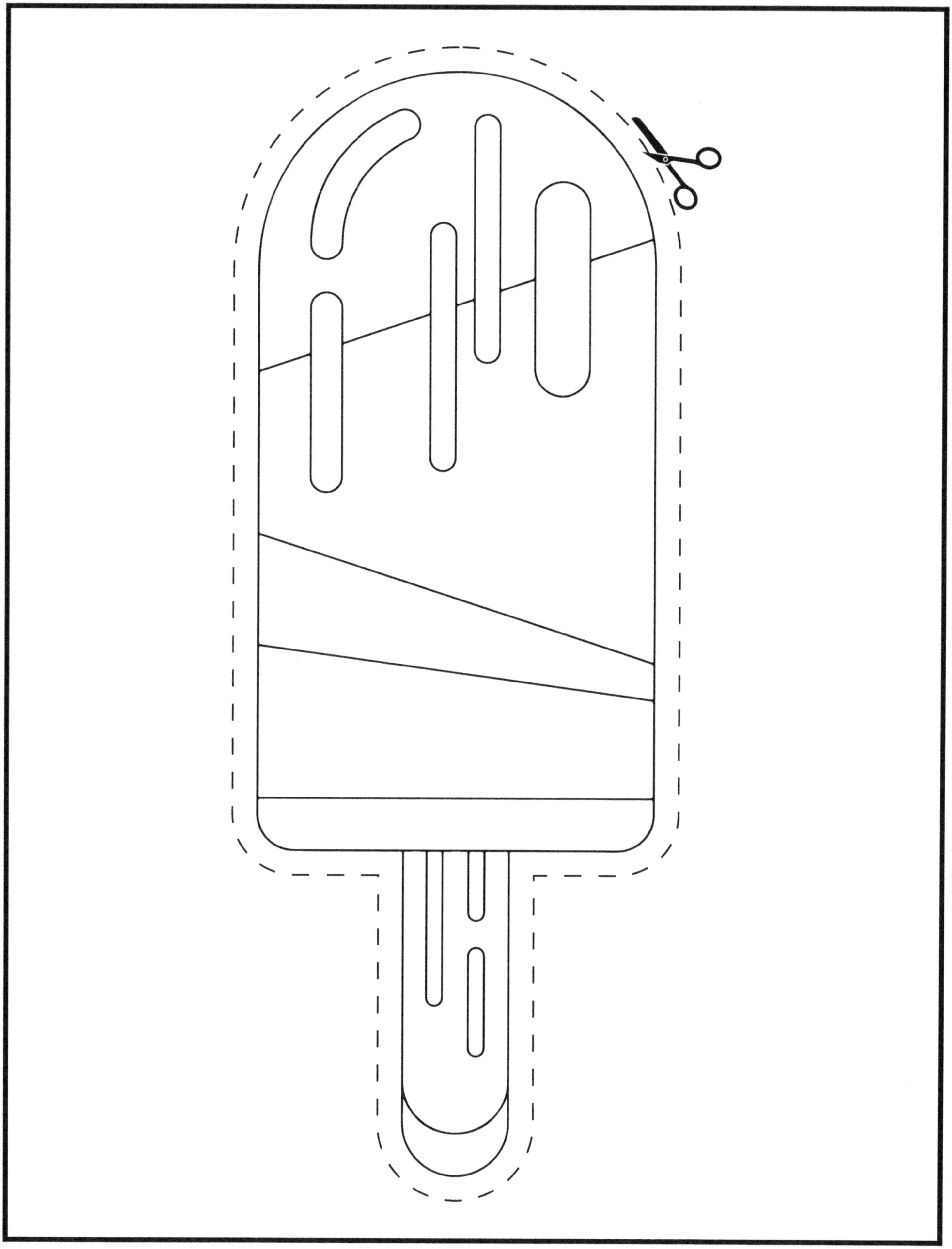

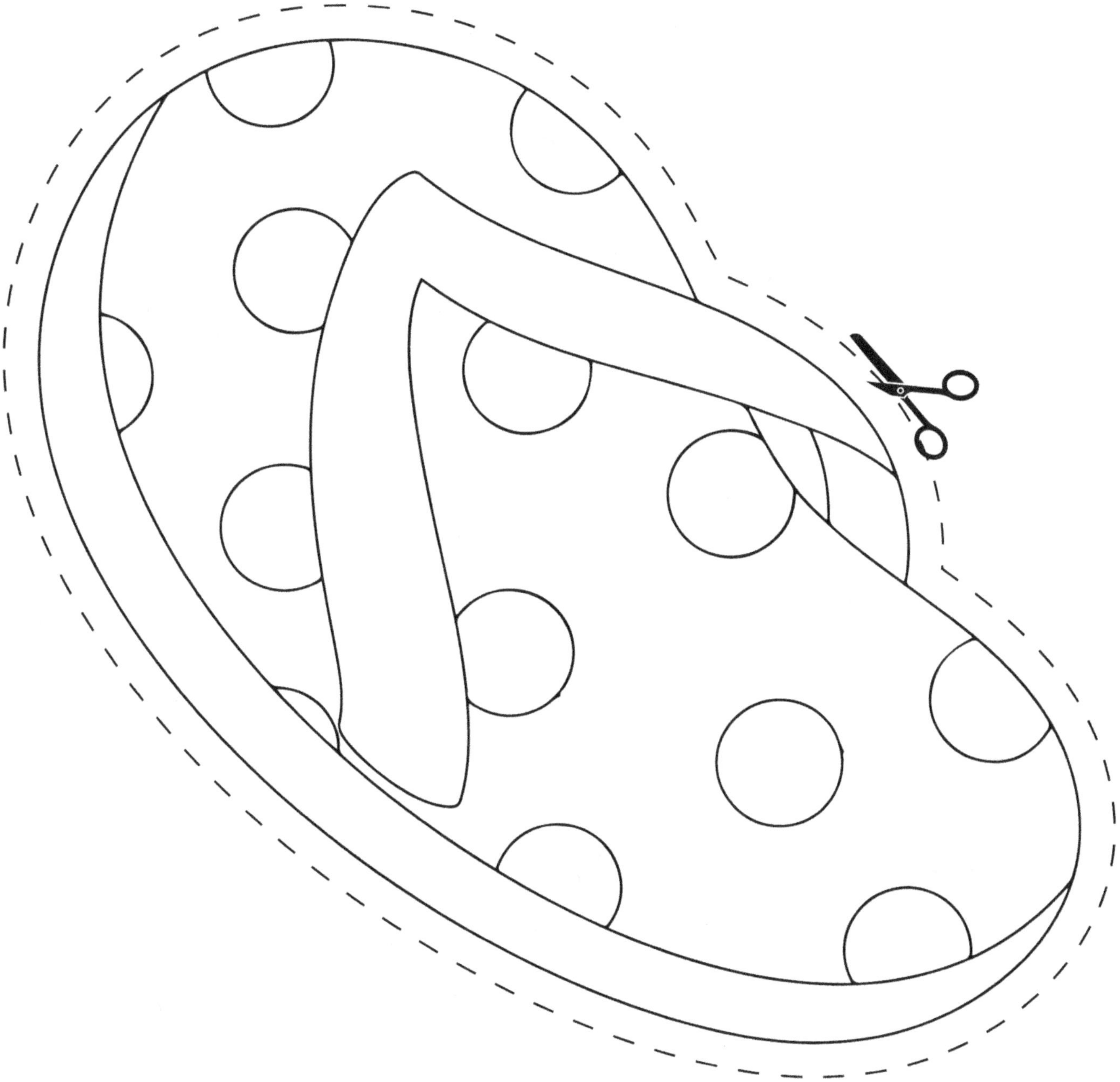

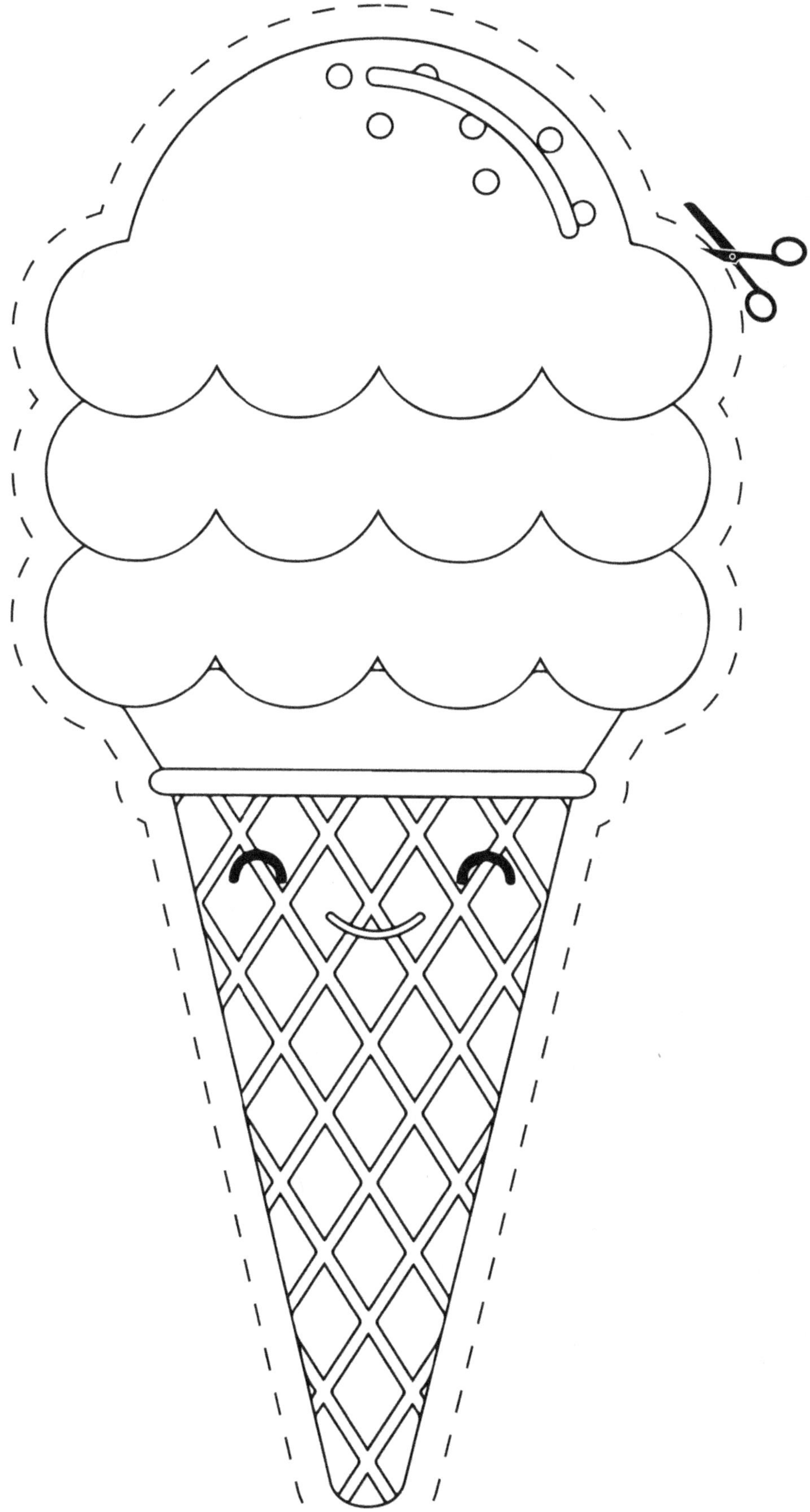

Gracias por elejirnos

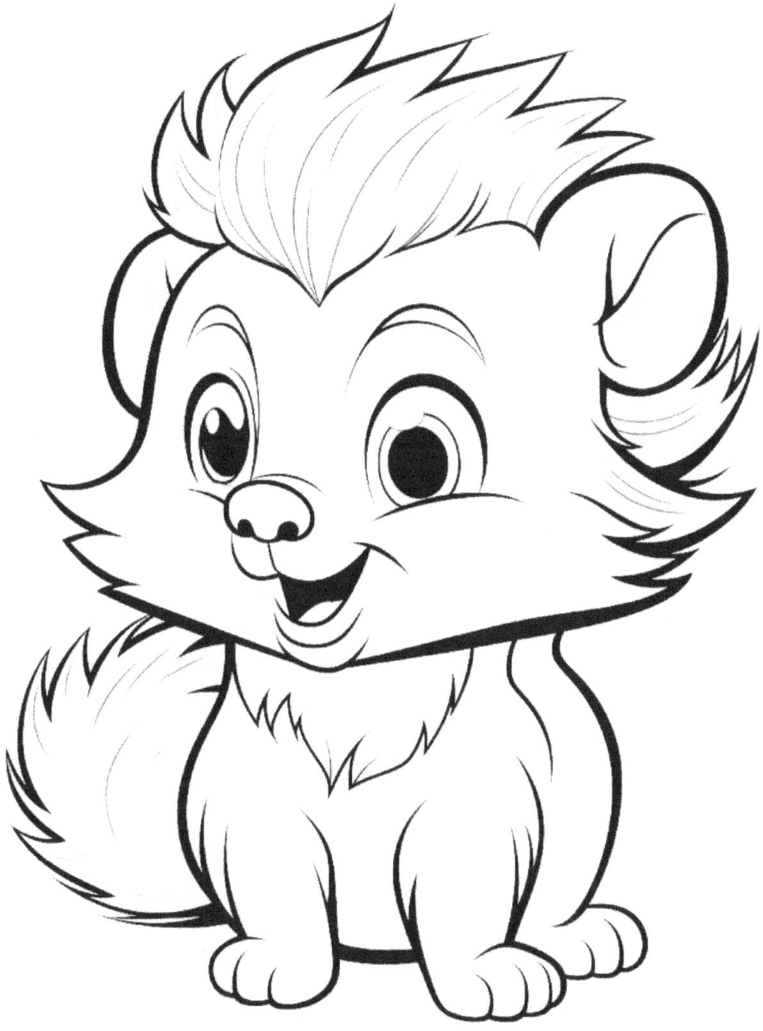

www.ingramcontent.com/pod-product-compliance
Lightning Source LLC
Chambersburg PA
CBHW081020240526
45471CB00018B/3917